LET'S PLAY
THE GAME

LET'S PLAY THE GAME

Collaborative Activities and Games

Charalee Graydon

With contributions from Sarah Hague and Collaborative Global
Iniative (CGI) member Kathy Porter

Let's Play the Game is designed for use with the novel, *The Judgement Game* published by Charalee Graydon in 2013.

ISBN: 1515294137
ISBN 13: 9781515294139
Library of Congress Control Number: 2015912517
CreateSpace Independent Publishing Platform
North Charleston, South Carolina

Cover and Designs by graphic artist Marsa Arbab and photography and art by Xesus Varela. Back cover photo by Dani Mandragora.

Let´s Play the Game is a collaborative project involving people from Spain, France, Iran, and Canada.

LET´S PLAY THE GAME

Overview of *Let's Play the Game*

Let's Play the Game is a book about generating ideas. It involves communication, brainstorming and creative thinking. It is about collaborating with other readers to gather and share ideas about social and legal issues raised in *The Judgement Game*. The issues raised occur in societies around the world. Your Collaborative Team (CT) is invited to share serious and light hearted moments when engaging in *Let's Play the Game* activities to solve the issues and problems.

Let's Play the Game and *The Judgement Game* caution readers to avoid making decisions about what is right and wrong. What is right today may be wrong tomorrow. Human history illustrates that decisions and morals are not static. Science and technology echo the same message. Our world is a world that adapts to changing circumstances and with modern advances in science, technology and ways of thinking, circumstances change quickly.

Let's Play the Game is a flexible game. There are no right or wrong answers, only ideas and discussions. Although some of the word games have right and wrong answers, should your CT decide to redefine a word, that is acceptable in *Let's Play the Game*. Changing definitions of words and laws can be done by the CT. This will, however, require a unanimous decision by your CT so the entire team is in agreement with the change and the reasons for such change.

The Audience
Let's Play the Game is a learning tool for book clubs, discussion groups, schools, colleges, universities and classes of creative thinking. *Let's Play the Game* questions are intended to invite group discussion. The reader and his or her CT decide when discussions will be opened and closed.

The Objectives of *Let's Play the Game*
The primary objective is that you are encouraged to enjoy the vignettes in *The Judgement Game* and the activities of *Let's Play the Game*.

The answers of your CT are gathered, sifted through and used to deal with problems raised in *The Judgement Game*. The overall obectives of *Lets Play the Game* are to encourage creativity and collaboration in responding to the issues raised in *The Judgement Game*. Your CT may have new ideas about solving problems.

Your CT's answers can be shared on social network sites, the member's site or on my website http//www.charaleeg.com.

Rules of the Game

* *Let's Play the Game* requires at least two players. The recommended size of the CT is between two and ten players.
* CT members must read a vignette or vignettes from the book of literary fiction, *The Judgement Game*.

* After reading the vignette, CT members provide responses to questions and activities in *Lets Play The Game*.
* CT's will have a facilitator to manage the activities and games. The facilitator can be either independent of the CT (such as an instructor or teacher) or part of the CT, being a person who has agreed to provide assistance in management of activities and games.
* Laws and principles to be used by CT members are those set out in Annexes A and B of *The Judgement Game*

Game Content
The vignettes in *The Judgement Game* describe situations of human problems. *Let's Play the Game* provides a forum for discussion of how those problems arose and an opportunity to gather and discuss ideas about how the problems can be dealt with and resolved.

Time Requirements
The CT or CT team facilitator defines the time to be given to an activity. Some activities require more time than others.

For ordinary questions it is suggested that CT members provide answers in five minutes. This will foster spontaneity and the free flow of ideas. For questions requiring more time, suggested times are provided in the book.

Requirement to Share
Each member of the CT must share his or her answers with the CT. It is important to remember that both *The Judgement Game* and *Let's Play the Game* are human games. Matters such as miscommunication, control by a participant or participants, internal politics of the team and different levels of player motivation can impact the results of *Let's Play the Game*. Much will depend on the CT facilitator, the decision making scheme adopted by the CT and the degree of commitment of team members.

Unanimity or Not?
Whether the CT demands unanimity or not is decision for the CT to make prior to starting the activities and games.

Let's Play the Game does not require individual ideas become a unanimous group decision apart from changing definitions in *Let's Play the Game*. The requirement of unanimous decisions is an option for the CT. If the CT does not require unanimity, each participant of the team can have his or her own ideas even though they are not the same as others on the team. Alternatively, the collaborative group may decide to require discussion until unanimity can be reached, to vote on decisions or to accept the decision of the majority of participants. Other methods of managing the ideas generated by the group can also be chosen. For example, some CTs may want only to generate ideas and discussion rather than achieve a consensus. Other CTs may decide to seek consensus in resolving problems.

Winning the Game

1. Everyone who is part of the CT and who shares his or her ideas is a winner.
2. On successful completion by the CT of all chapters of *Let's Play the Game,* the CT is awarded a balanced human being which is found at the end of the book. To be valid, the award requires that each CT member place his or her initials beside the balanced human being. This is the final step to demonstrate the CT's collaboration.

The Balanced Human Being Award
When I was young, one of my favorite games was a game called HANGMAN. I and my competitor each drew a tree and a noose under which body parts could be added to the hangman design. Each time I or my competitor did not provide the right answer to a topic that had been chosen, one of our body parts was added to the sketch of a human who was being hanged.

✓ In *Let's Play the Game*, the idea of punishment has been reversed and replaced with positive messages of achievement using checkmarks.

I have reversed the concept of the Hangman game. *Let's Play The Game* is designed to be positive, interactive and fun. It is designed to reward creativity. You and your CT are creating a balanced human being rather than hanging a human being. Creating a balanced human being is not easy and requires reflection and thought. Similar to the hangman game, your CT may decide to create only parts of a human being. The creation of the balanced human being takes time but the final result provides you and your CT with a sense of accomplishment and being part of a special group, the CT.

✓ Your CT, not you, is given a checkmark each time it provides collaborative responses to a chapter of *Let's Play the Game*. There are eleven chapters and your CT is given a check mark after completion of each chapter. There is a final exercise contributed by Kathy Porter, a collaborative wizard with experience in mediation and collaboration. Your CT will also be given a checkmark for completing the Findhorn game CAR, CAR activity.

Enjoy the game and have fun!

Chapter 1

DANCING WITH A LEOPARD: CASES OF DOMESTIC VIOLENCE

What does "Dancing with a Leopard" mean to your CT in the context of this chapter?

_____

_____

_____

YOU ARE THE AUDIENCE

In *The Judgement Game* vignette Fiona had not received psychological treatment for the problems she faced in her relationship with Tom.

Does your CT feel there would have been a benefit if she had received psychological treatment?

Yes ___ No ___

Why or Why Not?

_____

_____

_____

In *Let's Play the Game,* Fiona has gone to see a psychologist, Irma. Irma suggested Fiona devise a plan to leave Tom without Tom being aware of the plan.

Does your CT believe this is a good idea?

Yes ___ No ___

Why or Why Not?

_____

_____

_____

If your CT says that Fiona should devise a plan to leave Tom without him knowing about it, your CT is asked to devise the plan.

Your CT is given $2,000 and twenty minutes to devise the plan.

_____

_____

_____

_____

_____

_____

For the vignette, "You are the Audience"
Was Tom trying to reach out to Fiona to help her or to kill her?

Help Her ___
Kill Her ___
We don't know ___

Was Fiona killed in this incident?

Yes ___
No ___

It is unclear ___

Your CT is asked to rewrite the end of the vignette:

"He was stabbing me. I saw the blood and knew it was mine. Tom was the only one who heard my screams. I saw him reaching out to me as I heard the sirens and weakness overcame me. I felt myself falling."

Your CT's New Ending

_____
_____
_____
_____
_____

COURT SUBMISSION

Is mediation a way that problems between Linda and Pierre could be dealt with?

Yes ___
No ___

If so, when should the mediation have been commenced?

_____

_____

_____

REBECCA AND DAVE

In the vignette, Rebecca and Dave, does your CT agree with Rebecca who said her punishment was not fair?

Yes ___
No ___

Why or Why Not?

_____

_____

_____

Does your CT agree that the mandatory punishment Dave was given was fair?

Yes ___
No ___

Why or Why Not?

_____

_____

_____

CLAUDE AND DEBBIE

How would your CT characterize Claude's relationship with Debbie at the end of the vignette?

Positive ___
Negative___

Please explain:

_____

_____

_____

A SHORT CT COLLABORATION.

From what you've read, suggest 3 causes of domestic abuse?

1. _____
2. _____
3. _____

Suggest other situations of domestic abuse.

_____

_____

_____

ROLE PLAY – AGONY AUNT/UNCLE RADIO SHOW

CT collaboration – (ten minutes)

Write a brief scenario for a case of domestic abuse (male or female).

Improvise an agony aunt or uncle radio show. The victim (one CT member) rings in to talk about his/her problem and discuss solutions with the radio agony aunt/uncle.

The 'listeners' (other CT members) call in' to give their solutions to the problem.

(thirty minutes)

The CT votes on the best solution provided.

✓ GIVE YOUR CT A CHECKMARK FOR COMPLETION OF CHAPTER 1.

Chapter 2

FAMILY AFFAIRS

SIBLING PLAY

Is mediation a way problems between Hank and Jeannie could be dealt with?

(Use the definition of mediation in Annex B of *The Judgement Game*.)

Yes ___
No ___

If so, when should mediation have been commenced?

_____
_____
_____

CAROLE, RON AND FAMILY

Please provide your CT's thoughts on whether the situation in this vignette could have been dealt with by mediation? (Use the definition of mediation in Annex B of *The Judgement Game*.)

_____

_____

_____

FAMILY DUTIES OF KADAR MOHAT

This vignette has been rewritten for *Let´s Play the Game*. The new version of the vignette is:

> I am the only child in the family but it is not my role to look after my elderly father. Father had not been a good husband to my mother who he had abused on several occasions. Given what he has done, I do not want to look after him.
>
> I am now living in Torcia where my life working for a publishing firm keeps me very busy. I am married and have two children, a boy and a girl. I have disassociated myself from my parents and my past as well as from the customs of my country. My children have never met my parents. I feel it is better that way so that my children will not be burdened with the religion and customs of the country where I was born. We are part of a new society, a world of technology and commerce. We do not need to live with the old ways.

In *The Judgement Game* vignette, Kadar had accepted the customs of his home country that specified it was his his duty to bring his father to Torcia. In the new vignette, Kadar has disassociated himself from his parents and his past and believes he has no obligation to bring his father to his new country. Have your CT provide ideas about how Kadar, with his new ideas, should deal with:

His father's medical condition?

_____
_____

His father's lack of close family support in his home country given that Kadar is his only child?

_____
_____

What does your CT think about Kadar's decision to disassociate himself with his parents and the customs of his home country?

_____
_____
_____
_____
_____

Which vignette causes you to symphasise with Kadar? The one in _The Judgement Game_ or the new version?

The Judgement Game ___
New Version ___

Was your CT unanimous?

Yes ___
No ___

LOOKING FOR OSCAR

Was the protagonist in the vignette part of a fairy tale?

Yes ___
No ___

If so, did the fairy tale have a happy ending?

Yes ___
No ___

The vignette ended with the protagonist saying,

"I am looking for Oscar to tell him I am not a Princess and he is not Prince Charming. I am a middle aged woman with three children and Oscar is a common toad without either morality or a sense of financial responsibility."

Have your CT rewrite the end of the vignette to have a happy ending.

_____
_____
_____

TRUE LOVE

The protagonist in True Love has not been given a name. Why would the author not give her a name?

_____
_____
_____

Your CT has the opportunity to give her a name. Please agree on a name.

Her Name _____

Provide reasons why has your CT has chosen this name?

_____

_____

_____

Summarize the vignette in one paragraph.

_____

_____

_____

_____

Summarize the vignette in 140 characters.

_____

_____

Have your CT discuss avenues for reconciliation between mother and daughter.

_____

_____

Have your CT identify the people in the vignette who are blocking reconciliation?

_____

_____

Have your CT identify processes that can be used to assist the reconciliation.

_____

_____

_____

Have your CT draft a letter saying why Mrs. Trace does not want any more contact with her daughter.

LETTER TO MY DAUGHTER (Ten minutes)

_____
_____
_____
_____
_____
_____

Have your CT define "true love" in the context of the vignette.

_____
_____
_____

✓ GIVE YOUR CT A CHECKMARK FOR COMPLETION OF CHAPTER 2.

Chapter 3

ADDICTIONS AND OBSESSIONS

Have your CT discuss the difference between addictions and obsessions.

_____

_____

_____

In each of the vignettes of this chapter, an offender has an addiction or obsession.

What was the addition or obsession of the offender in:

Roses for Vicky _____

Beware of Betty _____

Reg's Repentance _____

Darlene's Dilemma _____

In your CT's opinion, could these offences have been dealt with other than by laying criminal charges against the offender?

Roses for Vicky: Yes ___ No ___

If so, what other method or methods could be used?

_____

_____

_____

Beware of Betty: Yes___ No ___

If so, what other method or methods could be used?

_____

_____

_____

Reg's Repentance: Yes ___ No ___

If so, what other method or methods could be used?

_____

_____

_____

Darlene's Dilemma Yes___ No___

If so, what other method or methods could be used?

_____

_____

_____

ADDICTIONS AND OBSESSIONS CLOUDS

From the list below, have your CT decide which things are addictions and which are obsessions. Fill in the words for addictions and obsessions in each of the clouds.

chocolate, cleanliness, cocaine, alcohol, cats, Valium, work, hobbies, heroin, cigarettes, comfort food, a pop group, a person, love, someone else, music, gambling, computers, gaming, books, shopping

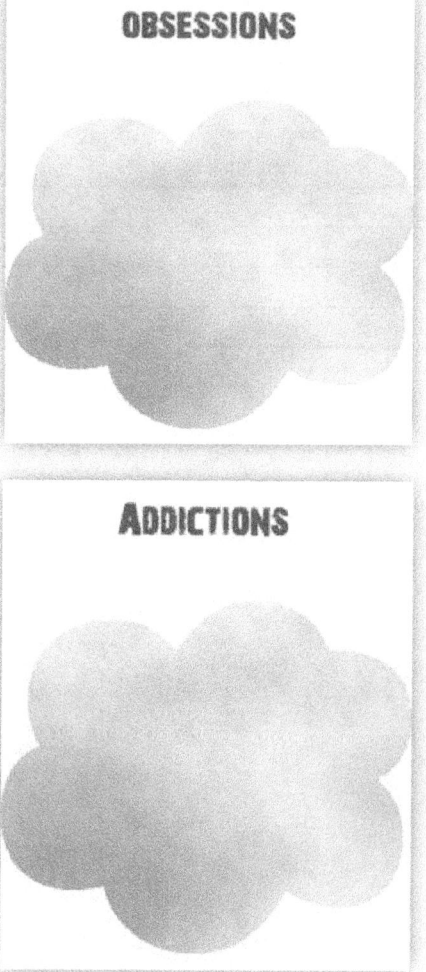

CT Debate (Fifteen minutes)

Addictions are easier to give up than obsessions. Discuss.

_____
_____
_____
_____
_____
_____

Please review the Stalking Law in Torcia (See Annex B of _The Judgement Game_)

Have your CT provide comments on the law:

_____
_____
_____
_____
_____
_____

✓ GIVE YOUR CT A CHECKMARK FOR COMPLETION OF CHAPTER 3.

Chapter 4

THE OMNIPOTENT DECISION MAKER AND CHAPTER 8: IMPAIRED DRIVING OFFENCES

Torcia wants to develop a drink/driving campaign.

Each CT member is given one of the following topics:

Media, Education, Repression (policing) and Punishment

(The facilitator will create tags listing each topic for the number of people in the CT and place the tags in a bowl. Each CT member will pick a tag from the bowl.)

Each CT member is asked to write a brief report outlining the drink/drive campaign on the topic he or she received. (Ten minutes)

Each CT member presents his or her report to the other CT members.

After hearing all reports, the CT votes on which campaign would be the most effective to stop drinking and driving offences. (Thirty minutes)

TONY'S TROUBLE

Does your CT believe Tony had a bad attitude to the Court system?

Yes ___
No ___

Could Tony be helped by being sentenced by his community rather than the Court?

Yes ___
No ___

If your CT says yes, why does it believe Tony could be helped?

_____
_____
_____

MATHHEW'S PLEA

Could Matthew have been helped by being sentenced by his community rather than the Court?

Yes ___
No ___

If your CT said yes, why does your CT believe he could be helped?

_____
_____

Compare Tony's Trouble with Matthew's Plea.
For which offender does your CT have more sympathy?

Tony ___
Matthew _____

Why?

_____

_____

RECIDIVISM AND LIES – A REVOLVING DOOR

Could the offences in this vignette, assault and uttering a death threat, have been dealt with by the offender's community rather than by the Court?

Yes ___
No ___

What benefit would there be in having the community deal with the offences rather than the Court?

_____

_____

_____

✓ GIVE YOUR CT A CHECKMARK FOR COMPLETION OF THE ISSUES IN THESE CHAPTERS.

Chapter 5

BOYS AND GIRLS BEHIND BARS

JOHNNY'S STORY: NATIONAL NEWS REPORT

Canvass with the members of your CT whether they have read news reports like this before?

Yes ___
No ___

What is your CT's response to the news report?

_____

_____

MOVING OUT

Victor posed a risk in the prison where he was incarcerated. Provide your CT's suggestions as to how the prison service should deal with this situation:

* Send Victor to a different prison far from his home prison with the same security level.___
* Send Victor to a different prison close to his home prison with a higher security level.___

* Keep Victor in his home prison with more restrictions. ___
* Other Suggestions: _____

A GAME OF MOUSETRAP

STORY AND QUESTIONS FOR THE COLLABORATIVE TEAM

George was a lawyer who handled cases for prison inmates. George received a call from an inmate at the prison indicating the inmate wanted to schedule an appointment with George. The inmate said he wanted to bring charges against a guard at the prison who has assaulted him and other inmates. He said there was a photo George needed to see and that he would tell George the whole story when George came to the prison.

When George attended the prison to meet the inmate, the prison officer on duty suggested that George take extra precaution to the lawyer's interview room and showed George a panic button necklace which he suggested George wear. The officer indicated it would be wise to take the necklace in the event that the inmate decided to take George hostage. George could not understand this request because he had been meeting inmates for several years without taking any special protection. What had changed?

The officer went on to say: "The prison service needs to be able to show what can happen when a lawyer takes the risk of meeting with these dangerous offenders. You have been meeting with several offenders that are unpredictable and dangerous. I am suggesting that you should take some extra protection with you when you go to the interview room. I'm telling you this for your own safety."

George focused on the guard's words: "<u>The prison service needs to be able to show what can happen</u> when a lawyer takes the risk of meeting with these dangerous offenders." Was the officer warning George that something was going to happen?

George knew that lawyers' conversations with inmates were intercepted by the prison service. The service would have heard there were allegations that a guard had assaulted inmates including the inmate who called George. The service would also have heard there was photo evidence of the assault that was to be provided to George.

George's mind envisaged the news report: "Guard at High Maximum Prison shoots inmate and lawyer in attempt to stop hostage taking"!

We know mice live in the prisons and generally scamper about freely. We know that from time to time, should a mouse scamper about too much or become too noisy, the prison service will set its mousetrap to catch the mouse. What we do not know is whether the mousetrap is also set to catch lawyers.

THE GAME

1) Was the panic necklace a protection or a set-up?
Protection ___ Set-Up ___
2) Why?

_____

© Nathalie Tahy Ngoma

OBEYING THE RULES

The prison brought internal disciplinary offenses against four inmates, (called the yoga instructors) in this vignette.

One of your CT members was one of the Yoga instructors. The Internal Disciplinary Officer has asked your CT to comment on why Mel was assaulted. Which of the following responses will your CT provide?

* Mel was not playing by the rules. ___
* The response of the Yoga instructors was effective to solve the problem. ___
* Simon was our friend. ___

The offender Bryan was seventeen when he went to prison. He had been sentenced to serve ten years in prison by the Court. Does your CT believe it would have been better for the community where the offence occurred to have sentenced Bryan rather than the Court?

Yes ___
No ___

Why or Why Not?

_____
_____
_____

PRISON ATTRACTION

Again, in this vignette, the offender was not given a name.

Have your CT discuss reasons why the author decided not to give the offender a name.

_____

_____

_____

Please have your CT choose a name for the offender

Offender's name _____

Explain why your CT chose that name.

Reason for Offender's Name

_____

_____

_____

Have your CT draw this vignette in a series of cartoons. Discuss what is vital to the vignette and capture the essence of each section in one of the cartoons. Create a storyboard of your CT's ideas first and develop these in each cartoon block.

- ✓ GIVE YOUR CT A CHECKMARK FOR COMPLETION OF CHAPTER 5.

Chapter 6

DRUG OFFENCES - WAR AGAINST DRUGS

MARY'S STORY

Mary's art has been purchased by an art gallery for the amount of $500,000.00. Mary was sentenced to a jail term of two years incarceration on terms she receive drug counseling for two years.

What does your CT believe should be done with the $500,000.00 which was paid for her art?

* It should be given to Mary. ___
* The entire $500,000.00 should be given to the state to pay for her counseling and that of other offenders. ___
* The state should be given an amount to cover the costs of her two year treatment with the rest being given to Mary. ___

PETRA AND WOLF
LET'S PLAY THE GAME STORY AND QUESTIONS

* Petra met Wolf at bar where she was working. She had only met him twice before at the bar.

* He asked her to become a sales rep. for his company, Celebrity Shoes.
* Wolf explained that Petra's job would involve travelling to Geliva to deliver money and returning to Torcia to bring back shoes for Celebrity Shoes.
* Petra was a single parent. After her baby, Jolie, was born, her boyfriend had abandoned her.
* Petra decided to take the job Wolf offered her.
* When her daughter Jolie was four years old, Jolie asked if Wolf was a good wolf or a bad wolf like the one in the Little Red Riding Hood story her mother had read to her. Petra said he was a good wolf because he had given her mommy a job.
* Petra made several trips to Geliva before Wolf changed the terms of her job.
* Wolf told her that heroin would be placed in secret compartments of the shoes she would be bringing back to Torcia. Wolf doubled Petra's salary.
* Petra continued her trips to Gelicia and deliveries continued for two years.
* On one trip, Petra bought a Little Red Riding Hood doll for Jolie's 6th birthday. This was a trip where the shoes contained drugs.
* When Petra arrived at the airport there was a problem at customs. The problem was with the doll Petra had brought with her.
* The custom's drug dog sniffed the doll and ripped it apart but found only stuffing. The dog didn't find the drugs that were concealed in the shoes.
* Because of the dog's response, the custom's officer took Petra's name and address but allowed her to return to Torcia.
* The following day when Petra took the shoes and drugs to Wolf, she told him what happened at the airport.
* Wolf was angry and said she had obviously raised suspicions and he didn't want her to work for him any more.

* Three weeks later, Petra was arrested on ten counts of importing heroin.
* When she obtained legal assistance, she found out that Wolf was an undercover agent for a drug investigation unit in Torcia. She learnt she was just a link in the drug chain. People at the top of the chain had also been caught and punished.
* Torcia's legislation allowed the use of undercover agents for controlled operations. This operation was a controlled operation to stop drugs being brought to Torcia from Geliva.
* The police had taken photographs of Petra coming through customs with shoes on ten occasions.
* Entrapment was not a legal defence in Torcia so Petra had no defence to the charges. After discussion with her lawyer, Petra entered guilty pleas to the offences.

© Nathalie Tahy Ngoma

PETRA AND WOLF QUESTIONS FOR YOUR CT.

Are there any morals to be learnt from the vignette, Petra and Wolf?

_____

_____

_____

Each CT member is asked to rewrite this vignette using just 100 words.

_____

_____

_____

_____

_____

_____

Each CT member is to reduce this vignette to 140 characters.

_____

_____

Each CT member is to reduce this vignette to six words.

_____

_____

Each CT member is to reduce this vignette to one word.

_____

Have the CT vote on whether Wolf was a good wolf or a bad wolf.

Good ___
Bad ___

THE COST OF BUSINESS

STORY AND QUESTIONS FOR YOUR CT

The anti-crime brigade of Jervis arrested Sam, a twenty-two year old man suspected of trafficking in drugs. He was stopped by chance when police were responding to a call on a different matter.

When asked to open his backpack, the police found six hundred and seventy five grams of cannabis resin and electronic scales. He also had a significant amount of cash, $2000, in his wallet. Sam acknowledged the cannabis resin was his but stated it was for his personal use.

Sam had been arrested three months ago for possession of three hundred grams of hashish. On that occasion he'd entered a guilty plea and been placed on probation for six months with conditions he keep the peace and be of good behaviour and take drug counseling.

The police officer's search showed Sam had been convicted of possession of marijuana three years ago and assault two years ago.

The police officer laid new charges against Sam for breach of probation and trafficking in a narcotic.

Sam entered a plea of guilty to the charge of breach of probation and a plea of not guilty to the charge of trafficking for which a trail date was set. He decided to handle the breach of probation matter on his own,

The State lawyer advised the Court that probation service records showed Sam had not enrolled in a drug-counseling course, one of the terms of the order three months ago. Sam made no comments about why he had not enrolled in a course.

THE COST OF BUSINESS GAME 1

(PLACE A CHECKMARK TO SHOW WHO BEARS THE FINANCIAL COSTS: SAM (S) AND/ OR THE COUNTRY OF TORCIA.)

A possible jail term for the new breach of probation charge
S___ Torcia ___
A possible jail term for the trafficking charge
S___ Torcia ___
Legal fees S___ Torcia___
Police services S___ Torcia ___
Drug counselling S___ Torcia ___
Court services S ___ Torcia___
Cleaning services for Courthouse S___ Torcia___

Was this a good business for Sam?

Yes___ No___

Was this a good business for Torcia?

Yes___ No___

©Nathalie Tahy Ngoma

THE COST OF BUSINESS GAME 2

A citizen's group in Torcia raised concerns that citizens are being stopped arbitrarily by the Jervis anti-crime brigade. Protests against the anti-crime brigade intruding in the lives of Torcian citizens occurred at the courthouse when Sam attended court. Police vehicles were vandalized on the street outside the Courthouse.

Your CT has been retained by the Torcian state to engage in a collaborative process to address this situation.

What stakeholders will your CT invite to participate in the collaborative process?

_____
_____
_____

PLAYING WITH POSSESSION

In the two cases presented in *The Judgement Game* for the vignette Playing With Possession, the reader is asked to look at the laws provided in Annex B of the book. It asks that the reader look at the meaning of "knowledge" and "control".

Your CT may agree or disagree with the results of the two cases in *The Judgement Game* but what is important is how the Court made its decision about the guilt or innocence of the offenders based on the Court's reasoning as to whether the offender had the requisite "knowledge" and "control" of the marijuana plants.

In *The Judgment Game* the reader was asked whether he or she agreed or disagreed with the Court's decisions and about sentencing the offender.

In *Let's Play the Game,* your CT is asked to provide ideas about the concepts of "knowledge" and "control".

In Annex B, control is defined:

When the person has power over or directs
(a) the act and how it will be accomplished, or
(b) the place where an offence occurs.

In Annex B, "Knowledge" is defined
To be aware of a fact or information.

Your CT is asked to reconsider the two cases in Playing with Possession and indicate whether "knowledge" and "control" was proven in each case.

Case 1:

Control: Yes ___ No ___
Knowledge Yes ___ No ___

Case 2:

Control Yes ___ No ___
Knowledge Yes ___ No ___

Does your CT believe these definitions should be changed?

Control Yes ___ No ___
Knowledge Yes ___ No ___

✓ GIVE YOUR CT A CHECKMARK FOR COMPLETION OF CHAPTR 6.

Chapter 7

HOME INVASION AND BREACH OF TRUST

HOME SWEET HOME

Does your CT believe Ben was:

A good citizen? ___
A criminal ___
Both ___
Neither, Ben was only an unlucky man. ___

Was Ben partially responsible for what happened?

Yes ___
No ___

WORD SEARCH GAME - HOME SWEET HOME

All words can be found in Annex A and B of *The Judgement Game*

Two words that signify using reasonable force to defend yourself.

____ _____E

What word is used for the unlawful premeditated killing of person?

_____R

What word is used for the killing of a person without deliberation?

_____R

The person who makes decisions about the guilt or innocence of a person in court proceedings.

_____E

What words are used for punishing an offender to ensure that other people will not commit similar offences?

G_____ _____

What words are used for punishing an offender to ensure the same offender will not commit similar offences?

_____ D_____

Word used for the concept that the offender will be restored to a useful and non-criminal way of life.

_____N

A word for the person who is arrested.

_____D

What nine letter word is used to indicate the person was found guilty of the crime for which he or she was charged?

_____ED

What five letter word used for the court process where evidence is presented to the court?

_____L

THIS IS NOT A FAIRYTALE

Have your CT decide if:

Fonsilla was a good daughter?

Yes ___
No ___

Why or Why Not?

_____

_____

Was PC a good match for Fonsilla?

Yes ___
No ___
Why or Why Not?

_____

_____

Was Carmella a good daughter?

Yes ___
No ___

Why or Why Not?

_____

_____

Was Ramon a good match for Carmella?

Yes ___
No ____

Why or Why Not?

_____

_____

What was the motivation of Gladysa for her actions in the vignette?

_____

_____

What was the motivation of Elsa for her actions in the vignette?

_____

_____

Were Gladysa and Elsa good sisters to Fonsilla?

Yes ___
No ___

Why or Why Not?

_____

_____

Were Gladysa and Elsa good aunts to Carmella?

Yes ___
No ___

Why or Why Not?

_____

_____

WHOM CAN WE TRUST?
<u>Review the scenarios of Bernard, Manuel and Eric.</u>

List three reasons why Bernard, Manual and Eric could not trust the people they had given authority?

1._____2. _____3._____

List three reasons these matters should remain civil rather than criminal offences?

1._____2. _____3._____

BOYS AND GIRLS IN BLUE

A citizen's group in Torcia has raised concerns about proceedings available to the public to oversee actions by members of the police force. Your CT is asked to review the three proceedings used in Boys and Girls in Blue and suggest two alternative methods that could be used to deal with members of the police force.

1._____
2._____

✓ GIVE YOUR CT A CHECKMARK FOR COMPLETION OF CHAPTER 7.

Chapter 8

IMPAIRED DRIVING OFFENCES

The C-Mind Machine is a new invention in Torcia and has two functions. The first function is to analyze the breath of a person to detect if the person has consumed alcohol. The second function is to read the mind of the offender to obtain information about his or her thoughts.

As indicated in *The Judgement Game,* concerns have been raised by human rights groups that the C-Mind machine breaches a citizen's right to privacy. Your CT is asked to make decisions in the three cases set out in the book whether or not to allow the installation of the C-Mind Machine in the offender's vehicle. Additional information is provided to you that was not provided in *The Judgement Game.* Your CT may or may not believe it is in each offender's best interests to instal the C-Mind machine. That is what your CT is being asked to decide.

Lillian's case:
Lillian is having an affair with the Mayor of the City of Reda, a married man. Should this information be released to the public, it will result in the Mayor's wife filing for divorce and claiming custody of their children.

What is your CT's decision about installation of the C-Mind Machine?

Yes ___ No ___

Why or Why Not?

_____

Len's Case

Len knows the the C-Mind machine could help him stop drinking. He has been having crazy thoughts about buying a gun and shooting people as a way to show his anger with the problems in this life.

What is your CT's decision about installation of the C-Mind Machine?

Yes ___ No ___

Why or Why Not?

_____

Gerald's Case

Gerald believes he started his family too early and is too young to look after a wife and child. He has been thinking about leaving his wife and baby.

What is your CTs decision about installation of the C-Mind Machine?

Yes ___ No ___

Why or Why Not?

_____

✓ GIVE YOUR CT A CHECKMARK FOR COMPLETION OF CHAPTER 8.

Chapter 9

BORN BAD OR JUST A GOOD TRAINING SCHOOL

RICHARD

Your CT is asked to suggest three reasons Richard murdered the women.

1._____
2._____
3._____

Was your CT unanimous about these reasons?

Yes____
No____

What other reasons were raised by your CT?

_____

_____

Richard has agreed to appear in a documentary about his life. He will talk about himself and reveal whether he thinks he as born bad or not.

Each CT member is asked to write a text for Richard indicating whether he was born bad or not. (Ten minutes)

_____

_____

_____

The facilitator collects all texts from CT members.

The CT is asked to choose who will play the role of Richard. Role play Richard talking to the 'camera' about what he has done and why by reading from one of the texts randomly chosen from those collected.

Based on the text read, other CT members will decide if Richard was born bad or not by voting.

Born Bad ____
Not Born Bad ____

SUNNY AND GLYDE

Your CT is asked to suggest three reasons Sunny and Glyde committed the Goldie store robberies.

1._____
2._____
3._____

Was your CT unanimous about the three reasons?

Yes ____
No ____

What other reasons were raised by the CT?

_____
_____
_____
_____

Your CT is asked to suggest three reasons Sunny and Glyde committed the Stagecoach robbery and kidnapping.

1._____
2._____
3._____

Was your CT unanimous about the three reasons?

Yes ____
No ____

What other reasons were raised by the CT?

_____
_____
_____

CT Debate (Twenty minutes)
Were Sunny and Glyde bad children as a result of bad parenting or were they born bad?

Bad Parenting ____
Born Bad ____
Both ____

If the CT group was not unanimous, each member can make his or her own decision.

A NEW FACTOR

Torcia has decided to clone Sunny and Glyde and change the characteristics of the children using genetic modification technology.

Have each CT member list two character traits of each child that should be changed.

Sunny

1. _____
2. _____

Glyde

1. _____
2. _____

If any CT members do not want to change the children's characteristics, have him or her explain why.

Sunny

_____

Glyde

_____

FACING THE PAROLE BOARD

What information does your CT believe is important in making the decision whether Brian should be allowed to live in a half-way house after he served twenty years in jail?

* Brian's written information ____
* Psychologist's Report ____
* Social Worker's Report ____

* All of the reports. ____
* None of the reports. ____

LAURA'S LESSON

List two things your CT believes could have been done to have stopped Laura from committing suicide?

1. _____
2. _____

Was your CT unanimous?

Yes ___
No ___

What other reasons were suggested by the CT members?

_____

✓ GIVE YOUR CT A CHECKMARK FOR COMPLETION OF CHAPTER 9.

Chapter 10

DEFINING THE PROBLEMS

EVERY PARENT'S NIGHTMARE

Your CT is asked to decide which Torcian department or departments were responsible for Anna's murder.

*   Education Department ____
*   Justice Department ____
*   Health Care Department ____
*   None were responsible ____
*   All were responsible ____
*   The CT was unable to come to an agreement. ____

Was your CT unanimous?

Yes ____
No ____

If not, provide three different opinions raised.

1.   _____
2.   _____
3.   _____

Your CT is asked to respond to Anna's murder by providing ideas to reform Torcia's education and justice systems.

Have your CT set out three suggestions to provide to Torcia.

1. _____

2. _____

3. _____

RONNIE X

Your CT is asked to create two <u>ROLE</u> PLAYs for this vignette.

<u>ROLES</u>:

*   Ronnie X.
*   Ronnie X's lawyer.
*   Ronnie X's parents.
*   Shopkeeper whose cellular phone was stolen.

Each CT member picks a role from slips placed in a bowl by the facilitator.

<u>ROLE PLAY 1</u>: Each person makes an ad lib presentation for the role he or she is to play based on information from *The Judgement Game.* (five minutes)

ROLE PLAY 2: Each person makes an ad lib presentation for the role he or she is to play based on Ronnie X's acknowledgement he committed the offence and his decision to stop committing thefts. (five minutes)

Twenty minutes for each role play.

TIME TRAVEL WITH DAMIENS

Based on information contained in Time Travel with Damiens – Cyberspace. Each member of your CT is asked to answer the following questions with the objective of showing Damiens was guilty of treason but not guilty of sexual offences:

1. Who was Luscious Lorna?

   _____

2. What did Luscious Lorna want from Damiens?

   _____

3. Who was X?

   _____

4. What did X want from Damiens?

   _____

✓ GIVE YOUR CT A CHECKMARK FOR COMPLETION OF CHAPTER 10.

Chapter 11

A NEW WAY

Torcia National News has highlighted **Distraction Burglary** in recent broadcasts:

Your CT is asked to set out five scenarios where this problem is likely to occur and three ways to prevent distraction burglary.

Situations where the problem is likely to occur:

1. _____
2. _____
3. _____
4. _____
5. _____

Three ways to prevent distraction burglary:

1. _____
2. _____
3. _____

✓ GIVE YOUR CT A CHECKMARK FOR COMPLETION OF CHAPTER 11.

COLLABORATIVE MATERIAL CONTRIBUTED BY KATHLEEN PORTER,
Collaborative Global Iniative (CGI) member.

Playful Approaches to Mediation and Community Building

Introduction:

Collaborative games and activities enable parties to explore situations and problems in a playful, often kinesthetic and more holistic environment. Individuals may gain personal insights into the self, the other and the group. By solving unrelated problems insights can be indirectly brought to bear on the actual dispute, conflict or problem to be resolved. The impact of the projects is that groups of individuals, from families to corporations will be more adept at communicating, learning from one another and appreciating both similarities and valuing differences.

Goal:

To see, to feel, to experience, to hear and to be; we are all a valued part of the whole.

Impact:

1. Mediators and facilitators use a variety of tools and communication modes to assist in decision-making and problem-solving processes.
2. Parties to conflict and dispute resolution as well as community building processes are agile in the use and understanding of various cognitive and sensory processes that can impact the resolution of disputes and decision-making situations.
3. Parties will have other modes through which relations can be built or re-established.

Objectives:

1) To experience different ways of working and playing together.
2) To appreciate the value of interpersonal relationships and the different perspective each person brings.
3) To appreciate different intelligences, each one of which make a valuable contribution to the building of a mutually agreeable outcome.
4) To appreciate different communication and learning modalities.
5) To appreciate the challenge of ethical reasoning.
6) To bring a sense of play into the dispute and conflict resolution arena.
7) To recognize the differences and similarities between non-cooperative and co-operative games.
8) To build collaborative communities.

Outcomes:

Mediators & Facilitators will have an appreciation of different communication modes and have,

1. additional tools to engage parties in dispute, conflict resolution & problem-solving processes;
2. ideas for games that build collaboration; and
3. an experience of differing modes of communication.

Games are also an excellent way to build cohesion in a group of people as they learn to trust and work together.

CAR, CAR GAME

We will play the classic Findhorn Game CAR, CAR. This activity will help you experience how you feel about trust. Trust and responsibility are two very important qualities in creating world peace.

Choose a partner. This is a silent exercise.

One person, 'the car', stands in front with his or her eyes closed and hands held in front of the chest with palms outward as your bumpers. The second person, 'the driver', with eyes open, stands behind with hands on the shoulders of the car. Keeping his/her eyes open, the driver will steer the sightless car around the area, avoiding collisions with other pairs. Remember that the safety of the other person is your responsibility, so you must show compassion and care. Demonstrate with one volunteer - compassionate, slow 'driving,' reminding the group that anyone with eyes closed is going to feel nervous.

The facilitator plays quiet music, reminds everyone about no talking and announces in a loud voice, "Begin." After 3-4 minutes the facilitator announces, "Stop. Open your eyes, and switch roles with your partner."

At the end, everyone will sit or stand in pairs and talk about how they felt in both roles, as the car and as the driver. If it is a small group, they can sit in a circle and share their experiences. This debriefing of the event is a very important part of the learning process.

- ✓ GIVE YOUR CT A CHECKMARK FOR COMPLETION OF THIS ACTIVITY.

CONGRATULATIONS ON YOUR COLLABORATIVE WORK
YOUR CT IS AWARDED A BALANCED HUMAN BEING!

YOUR FINAL ACT OF COLLABORATION IS FOR EACH CT MEMBER
TO SIGN THE BALANCED HUMAN BEING THE CT HAS BEEN
AWARDED.

BOOKS OF INTEREST

* Group Genius, The Creative Power of Collaboration, Keith Sawyer (2008)
* Creative Conspiracy: The New Rules of Breakthrough Collaboration, Leigh Thompson (2013)
* Read, Aim, Excel! The Expert Insights Weekly Guide to Personal and Professional Leadership, Chris Wallace editor (2011)
* Power Through Collaboration: The Formula For Success in Challenging Situations, Stephen Willis PhD (2013)
* Power Through Collaboration, When to Collaborate, Negotiate or Dominate, Stephen Willis, PhD. www.willlisllc.com (2012)

SUGGESTED FURTHER READING

* Breakthrough to Yes: Unlocking the Possible within a Culture of Collaboration, (to be released February, 2016) David Savage, member of Collaborative Global Iniative.

COMMENT FOR LET'S PLAY THE GAME from David B. Savage author of *Breakthrough to Yes: Unlocking the Possible within a Culture of Collaboration*

"Today, our world, our nations, our communities, our families, our organizations and our planet are faced with complex challenges that present massive potential risks. We are also at a time in human history where we are educated and connected, and have resources available like never before at our disposal.

With respect to the former, conflict, misunderstanding, misalignment of organizations and their leadership, lost productivity, wasted time and wasted resources resulting from limiting perspectives, distraction and hard-line positions are damaging our today and our future.

With respect to the latter, working together is a key strategic advantage for those leaders and organizations that build a culture of collaboration.

With her new book "Let's Play the Game", my long time friend and fellow member of the Collaborative Global Initiative, Charalee Graydon, offers a creative pathway to learning better ways to be in relationship that serve our world well."

BIOGRAPHY - CHARALEE GRAYDON, BA, LLB, BCL (OXON)

Charalee Graydon was born in Alberta, Canada. She is a writer, academic and past lawyer. She is involved in mediation and collaborative iniatives.

Charalee holds degrees in arts and law. Following receipt of a Rhodes scholarship in 1982, she pursued postgraduate legal studies in Oxford, England. She held academic positions in England, New Zealand, and Canada and has practiced law in Canada. She developed programs for students, judges, and the public on legal issues and published academic works on crime and punishment. She created and taught a course at the University of Alberta on sentencing and has given radio and television interviews on this topic. She published a book of literary fiction, *The Judgement Game* for which *Let's Play The Game*, her second book, is a companion. Her upcoming book *Can We Save The Human Race?* will be released shortly.

BIOGRAPHY - SARAH HAGUE

Sarah was born near London and has a degree in Arabic & Islamic Studies from Exeter University and a Masters in European Business Administration from the University of the West of England, Bristol. She arrived in France in 1989 on a romantic adventure and ended up staying there.

Sarah is an InterNations Ambassador for the Montpellier group, and it was during one of their events that she met Charalee Graydon. As a result of this meeting, she read and wrote a review of The Judgement Game, and participated in the French launch.

Sarah enjoys writing and is a frequent blogger. She began writing educational resources for children with Bongo LLP in 2009, starting with the Royal Albert Hall's 'Showtime', the Teenage Cancer Trust, and Webplay, and more recently a set of philosophy activities called Teatime Philosophy, and has written two books for children. Her work can be found at www.myresourcecloud.net

She is a regular contributor to the magazine BBBMidi about living in Languedoc.

Her blog, St Bloggie de Riviere, was created in 2005 and can be found at www.sarahhague.com

In her spare time, she enjoys exploring the countryside on a motorbike.

BIOGRAPHY - KATHLEEN PORTER, B.P.E

Kathleen is a Mediator and Collaborative Wizard who facilitates sessions with communities, associations, businesses and government agencies or any group of two or more with a problem to solve, a dispute to settle or a conflict to resolve. Over the years she has worked in Canada and abroad with scientists, health care, education, social service and business professionals, union members and managers to bring a sense of shared effort, joy and the more than occasional "Ah Ha" to groups engaged in the exploration of difficult issues or in learning new skills. She has worked in the transportation, health, recreation, education, and food processing industries and with children and families.

BIOGRAPHY – MARSA ARBAB
– GRAPHIC DESIGNER

Marsa Arbab is an Iranian graphic designer. She has a degree from Alzarhra university in Tehran. She works for Zoraq, a travel consulting company. Her work has been published in several countries in Asia and Europe. She has worked with festivals of travel and culture in Iran and is presently working with a European company.

ACKNOWLEDGMENTS

Guidance, friendship and assistance from Xesus Varela and Idoia Martin Ugalde. Encouragement from university professors and teachers who suggested this book be written and Collaborative Global Iniative (CGI) members for inspiring my vision of using collaboration to resolve issues raised in *The Judgement Game*.

DEDICATION

For family and friends.

www.ingramcontent.com/pod-product-compliance
Lightning Source LLC
Chambersburg PA
CBHW070844180526
45168CB00002B/953